A Woman

Without

a Country

A WOMAN WITHOUT A COUNTRY

Poems

EAVAN BOLAND

W. W. NORTON & COMPANY

Independent Publishers Since 1923

New York ~ London

Copyright © 2014 by Eavan Boland
First American Edition 2014

For information about permission to reproduce selections from this book, write to
Permissions, W. W. Norton & Company, Inc., 500 Fifth Avenue, New York, NY 10110

For information about special discounts for bulk purchases, please contact
W. W. Norton Special Sales at specialsales@wwnorton.com or 800-233-4830

Manufacturing by Courier Westford
Book design by Fearn Cutler de Vicq
Production manager: Julia Druskin

Library of Congress Cataloging-in-Publication Data

Boland, Eavan.
[Poems. Selections]
A woman without a country : poems / Eavan Boland. — First American edition.
pages ; cm
ISBN 978-0-393-24444-1 (hardcover)
I. Title.
PR6052.O35A6 2014
821'.914—dc23
2014030073

ISBN 978-0-393-35294-8 pbk.

W. W. Norton & Company, Inc., 500 Fifth Avenue, New York, N.Y. 10110
www.wwnorton.com
W. W. Norton & Company Ltd., Castle House, 75/76 Wells Street,
London W1T 3QT

2 3 4 5 6 7 8 9 0

The outsider will say, "in fact, as a woman,
I have no country."

—VIRGINIA WOOLF, *Three Guineas* (1938)

Contents

Acknowledgments

Acknowledgments are made to the editors of the following publications in which some of these poems appeared.

The New Yorker: "The Lost Art of Letter Writing"

The Yale Review: "An Irish Georgic," "For That Called Body Is a Portion of Soul," "The Moving Statue"

Threepenny Review: "Nostalgia"

Tin House: "Talking to My Daughter Late at Night," "An Island of Daughters"

The New Republic: "As"

Poetry: "Cityscape," "The Long Evenings of Their Leave-takings," "A Woman Without a Country"

PN Review: "A Woman Without a Country" (sequence)

The American Scholar: "Rereading Oliver Goldsmith's *The Deserted Village* in a Changed Ireland"

The Guardian: "The Long Evenings of Their Leave-takings"

Ploughshares: "Art of Empire"

"Amethyst Beads" appeared in the Academy of American Poets "Poem-a-Day" program.

"A Soldier in the 28th Massachusetts" first appeared in *Lines in Long Array*, the National Portrait Gallery's commemoration of the 150th anniversary of the Civil War (Smithsonian Books).

"Becoming Anne Bradstreet" was published in *Shakespeare's*

Sisters: Women Writers Bridge Five Centuries published by the Folger Library in 2012.

"A Wife's Lament" was published in *The Word Exchange: Anglo-Saxon Poems in Translation* (W. W. Norton).

"The Port of New York: 1956" first appeared in *A Poetic Celebration of the Hudson River* sponsored by the Port Authority of New York (Carcanet Press).

My thanks to Jill Bialosky, Kevin Casey, Michael Schmidt, and Jody Allen-Randolph.

SONG AND ERROR

The Lost Art of Letter Writing

The ratio of daylight to handwriting
Was the same as lace making to eyesight.
The paper was so thin it skinned air.

The hand was fire and the page tinder.
Everything burned away except the one
Place they singled out between fingers

Held over a letter pad they set aside
For the long evenings of their leave-takings,
Always asking after what they kept losing,

Always performing—even when a shadow
Fell across the page and they knew the answer
Was not forthcoming—the same action:

First the leaning down, the pen becoming
A staff to walk fields with as they vanished
Underfoot into memory. Then the letting up,

The lighter stroke, which brought back
Cranesbill and thistle, a bicycle wheel
Rusting: an iron circle hurting the grass

Again and the hedges veiled in hawthorn
Again just in time for the May novenas
Recited in sweet air on a road leading

To another road, then another one, widening
To a motorway with four lanes, ending in
A new town on the edge of a city

They will never see. And if we say
An art is lost when it no longer knows
How to teach a sorrow to speak, come, see

The way we lost it: stacking letters in the attic,
Going downstairs so as not to listen to
The fields stirring at night as they became

Memory and in the morning as they became
Ink; what we did so as not to hear them
Whispering the only question they knew

By heart, the only one they learned from all
Those epistles of air and unreachable distance
How to ask: *is it still there?*

Talking to My Daughter Late at Night

We have a tray, a pot of tea, a scone.
This is the hour
When one thing pours itself into another:
The gable of our house stored in shadow.
A spring planet bending ice
Into an absolute of light.
Your childhood ended years ago. There is
No path back to it. There is
No certainty I can find
The *if* or *maybe* that might remedy
An afternoon you walked up the hill
After school. In winter, in tears.
The fire smolders down into cinders.
Lilac shivers in the March dark.
If love is a civilization,
As I once hoped it was,
And you and I are its living citizens
And if our words
Are less than rules and more than remedies
As we speak, maybe
Someone escapes from a wounded morning
In a small classroom and finds
The world is not stern, after all. Paper birds

Are folded and fly off in the playground.
And when lessons resume in the afternoon
The essay is easy. It is
A Day in the Life of a Penny.
Afterwards, at teatime, the sweets have old names—
Cinder Toffee Bullseye Marry Me Quick—
The children shout out and I listen
To hear your voice with theirs, but no
It's here now telling me
How late the hour is, the birds almost up
And we smile at this
As we put the tray away,
Douse the fire and wash out the cups.

Advice to an Imagist

Follow
the line you wrote
as if it were salt—not

the substance that was first traded
along sea routes
and sold for cedar trees
and silk, nor

the functionary
separate selves of sodium
and chloride,
married once

millennia ago,
that since became a shining
mineral mausoleum where

winged birds and fish
were laid down to feed
cruel kings on their way
to the underworld, nor

the old porcelain shaker
in your pantry that sticks
on rainy evenings and
won't pour—no
none of these,

but the word that comes
to the edge of meaning
and enters it:

What a man is worth.
What is rubbed into the wound.
What is of the earth.

Cityscape

I have a word for it—
the way the surface waited all day
to be a silvery pause between sky and city—
which is *elver*.

And another one for how
the bay shelved cirrus clouds
piled up at the edge of the Irish Sea,
which is *elver* too.

The old Blackrock baths
have been neglected now for fifty years,
fine cracks in the tiles
visible as they never were when

I can I can I can
shouted Harry Vernon as
he dived from the highest board
curving down into salt and urine,

his cry fading out
through the half century it took
for me to hear a glass eel
had been seen

entering the sea-water baths at twilight—
also known as *elver*—
and immediately
the word begins

a delicate migration—
a fine crazing healing in the tiles—
the sky deepening above a city
that has always been

unsettled between sluice gates and the Irish Sea
to which there now comes at dusk
a translucent visitor
yearning for the estuary.

One Thought, One Grace,
One Wonder at the Least

My neighbor liked to read late at night.
And late was late.
After dark, when everything was quiet
I waited for her lamp to straighten out
Asiatic lilies, lupin rows,
Lattices with their zigzagging shadows.

The moon rose, set. Our children slept.
A glowing discipline issued from her window,
Continuing past ash trees, hollyhocks,
And I follow,
I am following it
Back to a bad time on this island:

The Kalashnikov speaks on the streets
Again, the sniper climbs to his nest
Again. And my neighbor
Is opening her book,
The one she has been reading

All summer, the one she has been saying
Is best suited to the times we live in.

She turns the page. *Is the war over?*
I am wondering. *Are we done with this?*
All at once

A fatal kiss flies out of her window,
Fastens itself to a fuchsia bell.
And does no harm.
A famous battle, with arms, artillery,
A lame horse—and look—a burning village
Rides a beam of light until it weighs
A frilled fern to the ground.
But no one has been killed. Or will be.

The tears the new wife
Is about to weep
Because her prince is getting ready
To leave for war are falling safely,
Safely into a parsley bed.
In an hour or so, they will have lost
Their saltiness: they will be unshed.

And my neighbor, who died years ago,
Is closing her book, is
Putting it to one side as
Light slips down from the Dublin hills,
Leaving petals, bracts, even ash trees
Filling up with words,

Each one of them opening out
So language can find it, can save it.

Which is how I have always seen them since
Even though, as seems more than likely now,
I can never prove it.

Amethyst Beads

And when I take them out of
the cherrywood box these beads are
the color of dog violets in shadow. Then
at the well of the throat where
tears start
they darken. Now I wear at my neck an old stress
of crystal: an impression of earthly housekeeping.
A mysterious brightness
made underground where there is no sun
only stories of a strayed child and her mother bargaining
with a sullen king. Promising and arguing:
what she can keep, what she can let him have. Shadows
and the season violets start up in are part of
the settlement. Stolen from such a place
these beads cannot be anything
but wise to the healing arts of compromise,
of survival. And when I wear them it is almost
as if my skin was taking into itself
a medicine of light. Something like the old simples.
Rosemary, say, or tansy. Or camomile
which they kept to cool fever.
Which they once used to soothe a child
tossing from side to side, beads of sweat catching

and holding a gleam from the vigil lamp.
A child crying out in her sleep
Wait for me. Don't leave me here.
Who will never remember this.
Who will never remember this.

Nostalgia

When the cobbler shop closed in our village
with a hand-written note in the window
and an apology
on a wintry evening,
while crows sat with big shoulders,
their backs turned to the last shiver of light,
I was driven
not to elegy but etymology:

Ceapail perhaps, meaning binding or fettering?
Klabba from the Swedish?
More likely *cobolere* to mend shoes.

As if the origin of a word we used
without thinking could help us deal
with what we were about to lose
without thinking:

A small room
gloomy with machines, with
a hand crank and a leather treadle
where I saw a woman standing,

years ago, her paired shoes
in her hands and already
I was placing them in some ideal
river village
where someone said
I'll make up a bed for you

and immediately
I could hear the chime
of another childhood: a spare room
perfumed by windfalls in one corner,
porcelain ornaments on a tray cloth,
a painting on the wall of a flowered lane
I wanted them to walk down
until they wandered
into the dusk
of another word: this time *nostalgia*.

The first part of it, *nostos*, meaning
the return home.

Eurydice Speaks

How will I know you in the underworld?
How will we find each other?

We lived for so long on the physical earth—
Our skies littered with actual stars
Practical tides in our bay—
What will we do with the loneliness of the mythical?

Walking beside ditches brimming with dactyls,
By a ferryman whose feet are scanned for him
On the shore of a river written and rewritten
As elegy, epic, epode.

Remember the thin air of our earthly winters?
Frost was an iron, underhand descent.
Dusk was always in session

And no one needed to write down
Or restate, or make a record of, or ever would,
And never will,
The plainspoken music of recognition,

Nor the way I often stood at the window—
The hills growing dark, saying,

As a shadow became a stride
And a raincoat was woven out of streetlight

I would know you anywhere.

Song and Error

The old Latin Master is dying
Among almonds, mosquitoes, the drizzle of the Black Sea.
The Emperor has banished him from Rome.

~

Ovid I loved you when I was a girl
I hated my fair skin and freckles
My irregular eyes with yellow in the middle.

~

You were my laureate of escape.
You filled the peacock's tail with human eyes.
You showed me how to flee from entity to being.

~

You could transform women into water.
You made the funeral smoke from the mercenary's grave
Spiral up to become a flight of birds.

~

You write you were banished for *Carmen et error.*
A literal translation might be *poem and mistake.*
Better to render it as *song and error.*

~

Now there is no escape.

Seventeen species of almond trees are flowering.

Everywhere reminds you this is not Rome.

~

When evening comes a boy who cannot speak Latin

Reaches to light the lamp.

He holds a candle made from the pith of rushes.

~

He touches the wick.

The room brightens quickly.

He has no language for the Empire that owns him.

As

A squeak of light. Ocean air looking
to come inland, to test its influence on
the salty farms waking.

Mist lifts. The distance
reappears. In an hour or so

someone will say *crystal clear*
even though there is
no truth in it since even now
the ground is clouding its ions and atoms.

The sun is up; day begins.
Someone else says *dry as dust.*
But this is outside Dublin in
summer: last night's storm
left clay and water mixed together.

The afternoon is long and warm.
The branch of one tree angles to
its own heaviness. While everywhere,
everywhere it continues: language
crossing the impossible
with the proverbial—

until no one any longer wants
a world where *as* is not preferred
to its absence. Nor a fiddle not fit,
nor a whistle not clean,
nor rain not right again.

I am walking home. A quarter moon
rises in the whitebeams.
At the next turn houses appear,
mine among them.

I walk past leaves,
grass, one bicycle. I put my key in the lock.

In a little while I will say *safe as*.

A Woman Without a Country

*This sequence is dedicated to those who lost
a country, not by history or inheritance, but
through a series of questions to which they could
find no answer.*

Sea Change

What did he leave me, my grandfather,
Who lost his life in a spring tempest
At the Chaussée des Pierres Noires
At the edge of Biscay?

With his roof of half-seen stars
His salty walls rising high and higher
To the last inch of the horizon
He built nothing that I could live in.

His door of cresting water,
His low skies skidding on the waves
His seaman's windows giving on
Iridiscent plankton never amounted to home,

And no one lay at night
Seeing these unfold in their minds with
That instinct of amendment history allows
Instead of memory.

I was born in a place, or so it seemed,
Where every inch of ground
Was a new fever or a field soaked
To its grassy roots with remembered hatreds.

Where even if I turned to legerdemain
To bring land and ocean together,
Saying *water meadow* to myself for instance,
The distances remained.

A spring night in Dublin.
Neap tide on the Irish Sea.
To the north of here in the Garden of Remembrance
The dead are defined by their relation to land.

When he looked over the ship's rail at midnight
Into his ocean garden
All he saw was oxygen unfrocking phosphorus
Lacing the sea with greens.

My grandmother lived outside history. And she
died there. A thirty-one-year-old woman, with five
daughters, facing death in a hospital far from her
home—I doubt that anything around her mattered then.
Yet in her lifetime Ireland had gone from oppression to
upheaval. And she had existed at the edge of it. Did she
find her nation? And does it matter?

Art of Empire

If no one in my family ever spoke of it,
if no one handed down
what it was to be born to power
and married in a poor country.

If no one wanted to remember
the noise of the redcoats cantering
in lanes bleached with apple flowers
on an April morning.

If no one ever mentioned how a woman was,
what she did,
what she never did again,
when she lived in a dying Empire.

If what was not said was never seen
If what was never seen could not be known
think of this as the only way
an empire could recede—

taking its laws, its horses and its lordly all,
leaving a single art to be learned,
and one that required
neither a silversmith nor a glassblower

but a woman skilled in the sort of silence
that lets her stitch shadow flowers
into linen with pastel silks
who never looks up

to remark on or remember why it is
the bird in her blackwork is warning her:
not a word not a word
not a word not a word.

LESSON 2

The death certificate I have is simply a copy of page 539 in the Registrar's book for the year 1909. Legally, she died in the district of the South Dublin Union. Officially, her death was registered there. In the margin, it is numbered 453. Name and Place of Death. Certified cause of death.

Studio Portrait 1897

She stands
on a fraction of paperboard.

Holds still
without shifting. She is

fifty years away from
the worst famine in Europe,

thirty years
behind the new nation

O sepia,
O stateless image making.

Where is the source of her silence?

Not history, our old villain,
you say,

but a muttering under black cloth:
those words

she listened to just a minute since
as the shutter fell.

And obeyed:
Keep still quite still not move not stir not once.

I wonder whether she turned in some corridor, looked
up from some moment of play and heard the whispers
and gossip. Did she hear in some muttered conversation
the future of an armed struggle, the music of anger, the
willingness to die? I doubt it. If she looked up at all I
believe she was listening for her life. And what was I
listening for?

The Long Evening of Their Leave-takings

My mother was married by the water.
She wore a grey coat and a winter rose.

She said her vows beside a cold seam of the Irish coast.

She said her vows near the shore where
the emigrants set down their consonantal *n:*

on afternoo*n*, on the e*n*d of everything, at the start of *ever*.

Yellow vestments took in light
A chalice hid underneath its veil.

Her hands were full of calla and cold weather lilies.

The mail packet dropped anchor.

A black-headed gull swerved across the harbor.

Icy promises rose beside a crosshatch of ocean and horizon.

I am waiting for the words of the service. I am waiting for
keep thee only and *all my earthly.*

All I hear is an afternoon's worth of *never.*

LESSON 4

I have come to accept that the story of Irish history is
not her story. The monster rallies, the oil-lit rooms, the
flushed faces of orators and the pale ones of assassins
have no place in it. Inasmuch as her adult life had a
landscape it was made of the water her husband sailed
and not the fractured, much-claimed piece of earth she
was born to.

I Think of Her

as if she had been made to drown
against the rigors
of squalls and wings.

As if her eyes were blinded twice,
first by a knife and then by salt
singing in the rigging.

As if she dove and rose with the bowsprit
her shoulders washed by phosphor,
her torso bare.

As if she had been made out of elm. *Ulmus:*
Narrow-leafed coarse-barked,
uneven canopy

of my courtship evenings
strolling Herbert Road with
my husband-to-be: as if she were doomed

to weep the harsh weather
of the Irish Sea out of carved eyes.
One loss promising another.

LESSON 5

She was not a heroine. She was not Ireland or Hibernia.
She was not stamped, as a rubbed-away mark, on silver
or gold: a compromised regal figure on a dish or the
handle of a spoon. Her hair was not swept or tied back,
like on the prow of a ship. Her flesh was flesh. Not wood
or ink or marble.

Anonymity

In the museum, an exhibition:
Women from Ancient Cultures.
Figures in glass cases, brightly lit.

Opposite, on the wall, explanations:
This was the wife of a king in
A valley rinsed by a wealth-bringing river.

This was a servant: see the flesh tones,
The beads. She was clothed in
An opulent fashion only when she died.

Reader be here. Go from room to room.
Note the substances
Used to transpose rigid stances,

Seized-up faces and the final
Splendor of grave clothes into these
Sign makers in fluorescent light.

Powerless queens; stock-still, enslaved
Girls at the entryway to anonymity.
Women without a country

Assembled from the treasures of a country:

A finger of silver. A mineral breast.

An ear poured out in bronze.

LESSON 6

A century on, I lift my head, I look up. The issue between an artist and a nation is not a faith, but a self. The issue between an artist and a truth is not a self, but an image. In an unrecorded existence she was neither and both. What troubled me was not whether she had included her country in her short life. But whether that country had included her.

A Woman Without a Country

As dawn breaks he enters
A room with the odor of acid.
He lays the copperplate on the table.
And reaches for the shaft of the burin.
Dublin wakes to horses and rain.
Street hawkers call.
All the news is famine and famine.
The flat graver, the round graver
The angle tint tool wait for him.
He bends to his work and begins.
He starts with the head, cutting in
To the line of the cheek, finding
The slope of the skull, incising
The shape of a face that becomes
A foundry of shadows, rendering—
With a deeper cut into copper—
The whole woman as a skeleton,
The rags of her skirt, her wrist
In a bony line forever

                severing

Her body from its native air until
She is ready for the page,
For the street vendor, for

A new inventory which now
To loss and to laissez-faire adds
The odor of acid and the little,
Pitiless tragedy of being imagined.
He puts his tools away,
One by one; lays them out carefully
On the deal table. His work done.

THE TRIALS OF OUR FAITH

The Trials of Our Faith

The Lamb of God was laid down once
On white satin, finished in gold edging,
Pressed into a vestment.

I listened to chains singing as
Incense rose to the glass-skinned, sea-green
Saints and martyrs.

Now in the half-lit, humidified
Air of the Museum
I lean over to see

A bruised Psalter
Dug up by a bulldozer in a Tipperary field,
Its thousand-year-old page lying open:

Yea, let them be put to shame and perish.

And now our Christian history appears
Rewritten on the skins of flayed animals,
The cured hides—

Their last cries sealed in this vellum
That has been freeze-dried,
painstakingly restored.

And will never heal.

The Moving Statue

There is always a first garden.
Learning the crab apple tree.
Hearing the word *shoo* for magpies,
and *dapple* for the first time.

Tended light lay every day
that summer enveloping
apple trees, bell-like fuchsias,
the low slope of an incline
five miles south of Kinsale.

Where in a tangle of spruce,
pine, sycamore, beside
a thick swivel of lilac
and a sign pointing to Cork
a statue of the Virgin stood
back from a balustrade,
the crown of her head haloed
with small electric bulbs
while blue concrete letters
under her feet spelled out
I am the Immaculate Conception.

While the familiar news
of guns in moonless darkness
and snipers at dawn
was upstaged by the story
of a woman who stopped
by a grotto in Ballinspittle
and saw a statue move.

It was a warm summer
The days starved of rain.
Soon it would be harvest,
time to save the hay,
holiday makers watching
their train windows filling
with the crop laid in swatches,
left to dry for hours as
the light grew less.

And the Blessed Virgin
in her accustomed place
harvested the longing
seen on warm evenings
in every upturned face
as the radio brought news
of wonders and illusions:
the Virgin's hands unfolding,
an entire statue rising
an inch above its pedestal

while a whole town abandoned
its fields and supper tables,
its nights of cow bingo,
the roads clogged with cars,
new visitors learning
directions to the grotto:
a countryside perfecting
its discipline of yearning.

Then the season changed.
Upstairs in my room,
the Dublin hills hidden,
I took down my notebook—
your eyes shall be opened—
and left the page unwritten.

Early twilights rested
on the incline to the west.
October dawns flamed—
A sword in the east.
By every news report
the Virgin's hands were still.
No movement. Not a gesture.

The Blue Rose

That summer,
the air cool,
the island out of sorts—

violence talked about on radio,
at dinner tables,
after television shows—

my mother told me she would be
in her garden
almost all summer

grafting new growth on
common stock: almost all summer
making a blue rose.

Nothing is left in my memory
of a summer
that promised nothing

except the ominous
end of it. But I remember clearly
that autumn when darkness came

to lend its cover to a killing season
seeing at last these
ill-at-ease petals

estranged from moonlight and still
related to it: outcasts
of metal, of steel.

An Island of Daughters

Always the same dream,
the one in which
I unstitch the gall ink
and script
from great books,
unbuild Georgian squares,
push aside the waters
the Vikings sailed
and find myself
at last on
an island of daughters.

In which the river, the millrace,
the mulberry trees
stripped of leaves,
stripped of history, the breeze,
even the war memorials
to who we fought
and who fought us
speak with one voice
about the sadness,
the remembrance,
the wretchedness of daughters.

In which there is only
monochrome on
the edge of evening, at
the end of the horizon,
not the thigh-deep grasses
of Ferguson, the magenta seas
of Mangan's dirge,
no refrain, no celebration,
just shadows
of women in
the shadow of a nation.

In which a girl
makes her way home in
the predawn,
to a street near the Liffey,
lets herself in, sensing
the blue air of reprimand
that goes with moonlight;
her foot falling
on the one step on the stair
that makes noise,
then a pause; then a voice calling.

For That Called Body
Is a Portion of Soul

On winter evenings, when she finished painting,
my mother's plain handled brushes
were left soaking in
a lost summer—

not in distilled turpentine ready to be dipped in
cadmium, alizarine, the colors of
skin and drizzle
but in this

product of sand, product of silica:
sensory transient of the process
of making the dense clear,
little jam jar

making obvious in alliteration its origin
in a hot afternoon when crab apples
were pulled down
from treetops

boiled in a copper pot,
poured into glass and left cooling:

a scalded jewel on a pantry shelf.
Only to be

emptied out again
filled with turpentine—
a winter emblem of dualities:
Even the crab apple is seeking

a sky of inferences to constellate with:
the rosiness of a larger fruit,
the hint of a sea creature sidling in
another element.

When I was expecting my second child
my mother turned to me. She said
Surely you don't believe
you're two souls at this moment?

An Irish Georgic

They flooded the Liffey valley years ago
to make a dam, water pouring
into fields, into sloped inclines,
into a floor of wildflowers before I was born.

During the years of greed,
of taking and dissembling,
that was the story that came back, the one I remembered:

Listen, who reads the classics? And who cares
whether a georgic works or what Virgil said,
or whether its meaning now remains good:

Join in my work,
and to my numbers bring
your needful succor; for your gifts I sing.

Listen, if you had seen what happened,
heard the details, knew what lay ahead of us, you would.

*

If there is an ethic to a georgic
let it be the down to earth and literal,
sifting, critical and absolute devotion to a way of life.

Let dirt roads rise to the horizon
on winter evenings in the Wicklow Gap. Let
the red-breasted merganser ford the same waters
the Vikings used to raid monasteries.

And now imagine a valley:
a tea-time clock, a silhouette of sycamores
a blue saucer beside its cup.

                    *

When everything failed
when ghost estates
wandered the Irish countryside, their windows
looking blindly out at rain I thought of this again.

Someone said *sluice*. Someone said *dam*.
Someone said *progress* and
the blue saucer drowned.

                    *

Surely the hope is a story can stay open
with its anthem of small details singing,
its cup still on the dresser

and all of it unfinished in this form
that needs little enough to become a hymn
to the durable and daily implement, the stored
possibility of another day. And nothing more.

Mirror. Memory

The man and woman in a formal portrait
before me in the gallery,
born to the high summer of Flemish pride—

pride in their eyes, rendered with animal glues,
in the elaborate loops of their collars,
even pride in the painter

who only yesterday applied gesso
and tacked the canvas to make them ready for
a future of perpetual intrusion—

are not the ones I want to remember:
winter provincials listening for infant cries,
boiling a kettle in the predawn,

their faces misted and revealed
in the steel of it, their moment passing,
passing; nothing but sleep in their eyes.

The Wife's Lament

Translated from the Anglo-Saxon, *Exeter Book*

I sing this poem full of grief.
    Full of sorrow about my life
Ready to say the cruel state
    I have endured, early and late,
And never more I will tell
    Than now—now that exile
Has fallen on me with all its pain.
    My lord has gone, has fled away
Over the sea. The break of day
    Found me grieving for a prince
Who left his people. Then at once
    I started out on my journey,
Little more than a refugee,
    Lacking a retinue and friends
With needy means and needy ends.
    They plotted together, his kith, his kin.
They met in secret, they made a plan
    To keep us apart, as far away
From one another, night and day
    As ever they could while making sure
I would feel anguish and desire.
    My lord and master made his will

Clear to me: He said, be still.
      Stay here. In this place.
So here I am—penniless, friendless,
      Lacking him, my heart's companion,
Bitterly sad because our union
      Suited me so well, so well
And for so long. How could the real
      State of his heart, the actual weakness
In his mind, the true darkness
      Of murderous sin be hidden away?
Yet I well remember a day
      Of singular joy on this earth
When we two vowed that only death
      Could sunder us. But now I see
Love itself has deserted me:
      Love that seemed so true, so trusted
Is now as if it never existed.
      Wherever I go, far or near,
Enmity springs from what was dear.
      I was commanded to this grove
Under an oak tree, to this cave,
      An ancient cave, and I am filled
With longing here where hedges, wild
      With briars, valleys, rolling
Hills all add up to a joyless dwelling.
      So often here, the fact of his leaving
Seizes my heart. There are lovers living
      This very minute who keep their beds

While I am walking in these woods,
　　Through these caves alone at dawn.
Here I sit. And here I mourn
　　Through summer hours, all my woes,
My exiled state. I cannot ease
　　My careworn heart nor soothe the strife
Of that desire which is my life.
　　Let a young man be sober, tough
And even-tempered however weighed
　　Down his soul, however sad.
And if it happens joy is his choice
　　May his self be its only source.
My lost lord, my lover-felon,
　　Let him be cast out alone
By an icy cliff in a cold storm.
　　Let his own mind bedevil him
With weariness as the water flows
　　Far below his makeshift house.
Let my weary friend beside the sea
　　Suffer a cruel anxiety.
Let him be reminded in that place
　　Of another home with all its grace.
And all the affliction, all the cost
　　Of longing for a love that's lost.

Marriages

When we married we brought little enough with us.
Letters. Photographs.
They made strange and went yellow at the edges.
And something else as well—our purposes of elegy.

They brought us to the small towns of an island:
Those worn-out streets
Wandering into a history we had never listened to.
We followed them even though we never found them—

Those windows growing yellow in a hundred dusks,
Peat smoke and the loneliness of roads traveling
Into a distance: lives
Without union and minds which could not tolerate ideas.

And the war memorial which reared up in the space
Provided by the committee listing battles in granite
From the local quarry.
Not our names. Not our wars. Never our victories.

They brought us to the long nights of talk ending in
The bond of another marriage—
Ectoplasm and air embodied in the way we promised
To join the place we lived in to the one we grieved for.

Which is how we found the green painted windowsills,
The limewash walls at the end of another road,
And inside a tenor voice singing
Words we had known from songs we were made by:

The cadences explaining our defeats and the sugared
Train of thought guiding us
To the last verse we listened to in the twilight:
The one that had learned us by heart.

Wedding Poem

On the occasion of the marriage of Eavan Casey to
Éamonn Barry, October 16th 2012.

Now on this day of promises
October light finds a way
To join the distance to our sight
For a moment that cannot stay.
As if to prove what we know:
There is no ordinary day.

Now on this day of promises,
One hand beneath and one above,
Each with a separate history,
Will join together as if to prove
The never worn-out covenant:
There is no ordinary love.

EDGE OF EMPIRE

Shame

So many names for misery.

One master.

He was the Master of the Workhouse.
Or of the House of Industry.
Or of the Clonmel Union.
Or of the poorhouse.

Which one of them can accurately render
at this distance
the brick, the old windows,
the ledger with its clearly written entries?

My father's father's father. Just that near.
Just that far away.

Just that name enough to make a sparkle
on the skin I could say was fever
and I know is shame.

So many beef stickings.
So much stirabout. So much oatmeal.
So many haricots in season.

Edge of Empire

1. THE HAT

1890. Empire, attitude.
A rainy afternoon in Dublin.
The Lord Lieutenant's escort
Rides to the Castle.

Shy looks in a cheval mirror.
Try-outs and *why-nots*.
A milliner scribbles in
the margin of a broken city,

Imitating the fatty
Outer layer
Of apple blossom,
The secret tongue of flowers,

A swallow's wing,
Fixing a denizen of air
At the hairline with
A mother of pearl pin.

The rain stops.
A woman crosses Grafton Street,

Her head a dialect, an argot,
A patois of colony.

2. READING THE VICTORIAN NOVEL

Today is Tuesday and the conversation
shifts to muslin, rubbed silver. Later
they will walk as far as the mulberry bush,
into the next chapter.

There is a parson, his wife's sister and
the squire has just arrived for a visit.
There are issues: a small accident
on the road last night.

I lean in to hear the words, a few whispers,
but something else, some other noise
is distracting me. It is, after all,
1858 and suddenly

the open page is the page opening and
without warning I am standing there in
the room with them in a blouse I put
on this morning in

a hurry, in an old skirt and in the shoes
I only use to walk in and they are talking—
this trio—about the benefice,
about the parish and I know

you will not like it, Clio, this menial task
I have in mind for you: speak for me,
say *history* say *famine*
say *fever* say *Trevelyan.*

But you are speechless: it is too late. They
never look up; they are wondering whether
the carriage wheel may have been the culprit.
I close the book.

3. NATIONHOOD: TWO FAILED SONNETS

Speranza—
on a winter evening
loosening her hair,
looking for the paper left
by the window: words
crossed out, words
to write down before supper.
January rinses
Merrion Square with grime, lets
the colliers stamp in late with
wet coats and coal, lets
the carriages finish up
their business of calling
and colony.

The dewy silence
of *Pax Britannica,*
its stewards sleeping
through a peace that
will never hold.
She is up late.
On the edge, at the brink
Above an underworld.
My country, wounded to the heart.
We should go now. She is
busy with
the transformation.
She is writing to Ireland.
Ireland. She is.

4. EDGE OF EMPIRE

A linen cloth hiding its past of beaten flax.
An empty claret glass. A plate pushed away.
An intimate aftermath that is also an absence.
A napkin twisted out of shape by the last hands that held it.

A round table, inlaid with light and marquetry.
A ruined garden lying outside, its fountain dry.
A rare plant brought from India, shivering and dying there.
The family prayer book laid just out of reach of forgiveness.

A Soldier in the 28th Massachusetts

If his cause is American,
and his gun British—

a muzzle-loading musket
made in Enfield—

the features underneath
the blue forage cap are

Irish: a rough-cut intaglio
incised in a hidden history

of a shoreline receding
into a rainy distance

that eased out in the end
to reveal another coast

whose leaves are turning
this September evening

by the green incline
of Antietam Creek.

And if this soldier in
the 28th Massachusetts is

to hold himself in readiness
for the reckoning

with his new countrymen,
let him not remember,

not once,
his old ones. Better to forget

the deep-water harbor,
the ship waiting, his father

on the dock with a contract
ticket for his wife and son,

weeping helplessly,
in the arms of his brother.

Rereading Oliver Goldsmith's
The Deserted Village in a Changed Ireland

1

Well not for years—at least not then or then.
I never looked at it. Never took it down.
The place was changing. That much was plain:
Land was sold. The little river was paved over with stone.
Lilac ran wild.
Our neighbors opposite put out the *For Sale* sign.

2

All the while, I let Goldsmith's old lament remain
Where it was: high on my shelves, stacked there at the back—
Dust collecting on its out-of-date, other-century,
    superannuated pain.

3

I come from an old country.
Someone said it was past its best. It had missed its time.
But it was beautiful. Blue suggested it, and green defined it.
Everywhere I looked it provided mirrors, mirror flashes,
    sounds.
Its name was not Ireland. It was Rhyme.

4

I return there for a moment as the days
Wind back, staying long enough to hear vowels rise
Around the name of a place.
Goldsmith's origin but not his source.
Lissoy. Signal and sibilance of a river hamlet with trees.

5

And stay another moment to summon his face,
To see his pen work the surface,
To watch lampblack inks laying phrase after phrase
On the island, the village he is taking every care to erase.

6

And then I leave.

7

Here in our village of Dundrum
The Manor Laundry was once the Corn Mill.
The laundry was shut and became a bowling alley.
The main street held the Petty Sessions and Dispensary.

8

A spring morning.
A first gleam of sunshine in Mulvey's builder's yard.

The husbands and wives in the walled graveyard
Who brought peace to one another's bodies are not separated.
But wait. Mulvey's hardware closed down years ago.
The cemetery can't be seen from the road.

9

Visitors come from the new Town Centre,
Built on the site of an old mill,
Their arms weighed down with brand names, fashion labels,
     bags.

10

Hard to know which variant
Of our country this is. Hard to say
Which variant of sound to use at the end of this line.

11

We were strangers here once. Now
Someone else
Is living out their first springtime under these hills.
Someone else
Feels the sudden ease that comes when the wind veers
South and warms rain.
Would any of it come back to us if we gave it another name?
(*Sweet Auburn, loveliest village of the plain.*)

12

I walk to the Town Centre,
I stand listening to a small river,
Closed in and weeping.
Everyone leaving in the dusk with a single bag,
The way souls are said to enter the underworld
With one belonging.
And no one remembering.

13

A subject people knows this.
The first loss is through history.
The final one is through language.

14

It is time to go back to where I came from.

15

I take down the book. Centuries and years
Fall softly from the page. Sycamores, monasteries, a
    schoolhouse
And river-loving trees, their leaves casting iron-colored
    shadows,
Are falling and falling
As the small town of Lissoy
Sinks deeper into sweet Augustan double-talk and disappears.

The Port of New York: 1956

What do we grieve for
when we leave a country
and live for years in
another one?

I was a child.
I came to the New World.
I neither knew nor was told
what I know now:

It is not the physical
or literal differences between
the ground we stand on
that marks loss

but what is severed in us
by the sound
of endings falling into
their lesser selves forever:

splendour for instance to *splendor,*
ardour to *ardor* ending forever
the hint of *dour*
with its harsh savor

and *catalogue* to *catalog,*
that elaboration
at the end of *rogue*
which made so many things raffish

and *harbour* changed to *harbor*
which robbed us of the *our*
by which we knew
no other city but our own

slipped out to sea in the night,
among foghorns and cormorants,
and came back at dawn
tasting of salt

Becoming Anne Bradstreet

Commissioned by the Folger Shakespeare Library
for the exhibition *Shakespeare's Sisters*

It happens again
As soon as I take down her book and open it.

I turn the page.
My skies rise higher and hang younger stars.

The ship's rail freezes.
Mare Hibernicum leads to Anne Bradstreet's coast.

A blackbird leaves her pine trees
And lands in my spruce trees.

I open my door on a Dublin street.
Her child/her words are staring up at me:

In better dress to trim thee was my mind,
But nought save homespun cloth, i' th' house I find.

We say *home truths*
Because her words can be at home anywhere—

At the source, at the end and whenever
The book lies open and I am again

An Irish poet watching an English woman
Become an American poet.